Praise for *Unwash*

"*Unwashed* gives readers the pure delight that people on Toronto's oral poetry scene have been enjoying for a while: the beautiful, profound poetry of Daniel Maluka sings and speaks from these pages with the voice of the poet in person. There is lightness and sadness, unflinching awareness and equal resilience in these poems that combine contemplative stillness and the momentum of story and song. I think of beautiful poems like 'Field Notes on the Hermit' or 'The Dream', where 'Two silent riders arrive at the ruined tower' In *Unwashed*, Maluka enters deep into the contemporary self while at the same time living fully, beautifully, often sadly in our world of tv dinners, John Lennon dreams, midnight regrets, assistant managers, cats waiting for a handout, social injustice, and the haunting presence of a father 'aware he sent his son into a world that hates him.'"

—A F Moritz

"Daniel Maluka's *Unwashed* is the unvarnished truth about the experience of feeling unwanted, unloved, and unfree in the midst of Canada's largest city. Maluka turns his eyes forensically on the lives of his family, friends, lovers, and neighbours, and on the conundrum that is Canadian Multiculturalism—so welcoming, so liberating—yet frustrated so insidiously by White Supremacism. These poems are scarily poignant . . . they are for all the 'unwashed'—not to bleach or brainwash—but to clear away the threat of whitewash with the promise of baptismal rebirth. Welcome, now, Daniel Maluka!"

—George Elliott Clarke, author of *Canticles III (MMXXIII)*, and Parliamentary Poet Laureate of Canada (2016 & 17)

"*Unwashed* articulates a coming into awareness of the junk enchantments animating identity and social belonging in Canada today. Daniel Maluka's voice lays down a story of betweenness—where one's sources of family and meaning conflict bodily and psychically with the foundational myth of home. A bid for tenderness permits hope in this first book of poetry."

—Dale Martin Smith,
Toronto Metropolitan University professor,
and author of *The Size of Paradise*

"Daniel Maluka's *Unwashed* stirred parts of my soul I didn't know could be reached. The emotions are so vividly captured, it feels like he's written a piece of my own heart."

—Carlos Anthony, author of *Shades of Black*

"Daniel Maluka is a keen and talented observer of the changing social fabric. These poems contain worlds."

—Moez Surani, author of *Operations* and *The Legend of Baraffo*

"unwashed   saying sew strong   daniel maluka sz

sure n trew lines 4 heering n reflekting who goes wher 4 what alwayze telling asking a brillyant vois daniel maluka compassyunate n sew stedee alwayze reveeling brillyant writing th genius uv saying showing how he n his frends n familee stay moov n change th lineage th longings th alertness n mooving th care 4ward brite aware n reeching langwage sew strong n carreeing all th lives daniel maluka writes abt sew adept n kleer wun uv th best books evr"

—bill bissett

UNWASHED

DANIEL MALUKA

poetry

MAWENZI HOUSE

©2024 Daniel Maluka

Except for purposes of review, no part of this book may be reproduced in any form without prior permission of the publisher.

We acknowledge the support of the Canada Council for the Arts for our publishing program. We also acknowledge support from the Government of Ontario through the Ontario Arts Council, and the support of the Government of Canada through the Canada Book Fund.

Cover art by Daniel Maluka
Cover design by Sabrina Pignataro
Artwork on pp. 4, 24, and 51 by Daniel Maluka

The following poems have previously been published as follows:

"Unwashed Reused" appeared in *Augur Magazine* 1.1, 2018.
"Willowridge Towers (God Speak)" appeared in *CAROUSEL* 47, 2022
"(Untitled)" appeared in the *White Wall Review* 41, 2017

Library and Archives Canada Cataloguing in Publication

Title: Unwashed : poetry / Daniel Maluka.

Names: Maluka, Daniel, author.

Identifiers: Canadiana (print) 20240364023 | Canadiana (ebook) 20240364031 | ISBN 9781774151686 (softcover) | ISBN 9781774151693 (EPUB) | ISBN 9781774151709 (PDF)

Subjects: LCGFT: Poetry.
Classification: LCC PS8626.A473 U59 2024 | DDC C811/.6—dc23

Printed and bound in Canada by Coach House Printing

Mawenzi House Publishers Ltd.
39 Woburn Avenue (B)
Toronto, Ontario M5M 1K5
Canada
www.mawenzihouse.com

*For
Agnes
Nelly
Moreny*

CONTENTS

Apartment Shadows   1
Form Four as Taught by George Elliott Clarke   5
Form Two as Taught by GEC   6
The Navigator   7
The Gears (Pleasure)   8
December 31, 1899   9
black dye   10
Mornings   11
A Word by Another Name   12
Bone   14
Travelogue   16
Goodnight at Dawn   17
Unwashed Reused   18
The Shrinking   19
The Dream   21
Willowridge Towers (God Speak)   23
Taharqa   25
Clutter   26
birds of prey   27
1:26 AM   28
Field Notes on the Hermit   29
Stillness   31
Familiar Tale   32
Around the Fire   33
Standard Repertoire of the Immigrant Genre   34

The Assistant Manager 36
Walk Hard 40
Here Lies a Brother, Friend, and Son 41
Father 42
Sister 43
Mother 44
Friend 45
(Untitled) 46
Myths Matter 49
The Arrival 52
What Forever Looks Like 53
New Ones Old 54

Apartment Shadows

we played basketball in the shadows of our buildings
dwarfed by the shadows of older kids
shadows looming over us and our buildings
swallowing us whole
I left early
but you stayed

in the distant heat of summers long passed
we braved the pressure of the beating sun
chasing after the ice cream truck
breathlessly thumbing through quarters, nickels, and dimes
the price of ice cream rose each summer by
nickels first, then dimes, then quarters

as the summers blazed on i would see you go to the Tuck Shop
using dollar bills to buy nickel and dime bags
I thought nothing of it

our school-day memories play back like videotapes
grainy 240-pixel videos in my head
on your walks to school your mother wanted you to stay close to her
you didn't
but I did
misbehaving was more your thing than mine
running from our mothers was more your thing than mine

you embraced the shadows of those older kids
I didn't
but you did
and stood in daylight with them

circling the area outside our buildings
like sharks
thinking nothing of it
I had things to draw

years lurched on, my visits to your place were rare
our call of duty zombie days were gone. I wouldn't even see you at school
your father gave a speech at our black history month assembly
he told us black men to
break the chains
you weren't there to hear it
you left early

I only saw the picture when I asked around for weed
and they brought your name up
I didn't know you were chopping

the night I came back from my first art show
I saw you at the bus station
I had moved away
but you stayed
in the shadow of our aged apartment
windows covered by flags and posters

you told me you were selling white cause there's no money in green
with no frame of reference, I nodded in agreement
you were still in the shadow of those older kids
often the place we lived
the neighbourhood we shared
comes up in the news
shooting here, stabbing there
~~murder~~

I would have a quiet moment for you each time
your father's words ringing in my head clear as bell
break the chains black men
you never heard them
why did you leave early?

Form Four as Taught by George Elliott Clarke

room curtains heaving
listening for changes in circadian rhythms. Waiting

seeking refuge from bickering personas and
rainfall thoughts.
stumbling through pen, paper, and day-long BIPOC workshops.
    Waiting

mourning at the graves of a thousand childhoods unlived
seeds unplanted.
hoping to gain a mentor's approval with letters sent in the post.
    Waiting

a life marred by the curvature of words unsaid.
the ravenous thunder of possibility, writing madly in moleskins
anything to avoid mediocrity. Waiting

the lights' potential extinguished fear
a flame holds no candle.
tell me I'm good

years spent in the shadow of the *dunya*. Waiting.

Form Two as Taught by GEC

2000 Chrysler Neon/ green venti
more common than taxes

than Irish Cream on
hot morning's weekend mist
and the golden touch

more common than empty offices of smart startups
on vacation nights in Manzini, we could
see them, in Swaziland stars look different

and Patrice O'Neal clips
on bright days draw humor from presidents
easier to inhale Lake Ontario through your nostrils

as common as grocery store sushi
and words of affirmation

The Navigator

when I was a kid, I thought my dad was a spy
he could speak French
listen in Portuguese
and ask about the weather in Russian
shocking me and Walter, every time our Chrysler Neon needed a tune up

when I was a kid, I thought my dad was a spy
he spent a few years in France
and would avoid questions—
him in Sanskrit and me in hieroglyphic
we were unintelligible

when I was a kid, I thought my dad was a spy
he knew our city well enough to drive without a gps
North York, Downtown and Etobicoke
but we were unknown to each other
too many left turns and dead ends

when I grew up, I saw my dad for who he was
willing to argue over the placement of a garbage bin
willing to ignore the smell of 3 am weed and Bacardi breath

when I grew up, I understood how frustrating it must be
to see your son make the mistakes you did
and to have him yield right of way to error
to have your warnings mistranslated

when I grew up, I saw my dad for who he was
aware he sent his son into a world that hates him

The Gears (Pleasure)

Desire can electrocute the body
igniting spine and sternum
powering on human lust
bodies sacrificed to the gears

blood rushes between heads
blood drips through the cogs
those gears control thought and action
until the urges are sated

whispers between the bodies
words splintering ear drums
skin rattling at the slightest touch

each person and their partner igniting each house of flesh
each house of flesh heated and dismantled
this house of flesh is dripping down the gears
this house of flesh lubricates the cogs

we reduce each other to a singularity
we reduce each other to mechanisms of desire
gnashing skins in fleshly rhythm

the gears lust for the automation of bodies interwound
within bodies interwound convulsing within bodies interwound
bodies interwound convulsing bodies interwound
value brought conquest and convergence

we are the gears
churning forward into what?

December 31, 1899

Dear Mountain Hermit,

the old ways are dead and dying
many a prospector down in Yuma done said the same
rushing gold rivers have since run dry
we represent a time long since past
like old musty garments of sown bison skin
we are discarded by the destitute
the sun done set on the west
manifest destiny has turned the other way
civilization is a heedless train
the phone lines tell it true
they are a scar on the land of the frontier

Signed,

Progress and its myths

black dye

porcelain sink stained black
attempting to hide ashen grey
lily white to charcoal
hoping the forces that rule time
see your point of view
small delicate strokes
one strand at a time
there is no turning
old stubborn men
life's winters spent
reflecting summers past
trying to outrun the past

                        fool's errand

Mornings

strong, stiff, and yellow
the odor volleyed in nostrils
owner standing over their canine
marking ownership of the oak tree

rustic, rich odor the
invocation of home
the coffee pot brings us
home.
nostrils rotating around routine

rotating bicycle wheels of mundanity
uber drivers clawing at their wheels
desperately shaking cages of mundanity
"I was an artist back home you know"

feeble attempts to escape, letting you know
of their flower-fueled John Lennon dreams.

A Word by Another Name

MAN
You would look better in a cage/Nigger
Worth less than nothing/Nigger
Son of worms of slaves/Nigger
Thieves and rapists/Nigger
My taxes pay your mother's bills/Nigger
You smell like government cheese/ Nigger
I'm the reason you ate last month/ Nigger
I put clothes on your back/Nigger
Your mother rules the domain of welfare/Nigger
Social Services is your middle name/Nigger
Yet you still want more ingrate/Nigger
You dream of rims and guns no more than a killer/Nigger

BROTHER
What we gonna do/Nigga
University is all a scam/ Nigga
How you gonna pay for school/my Nigga
Debt slavery is the new slavery/my Nigga
How you supposed to look fly/Nigga
How many bitches you hit/Nigga
How many stripes you got/Nigga
How many polos/Nigga
Polo none of that USPA shit/Nigga
Its time for you to help yo' Momma/my Nigga
School ain't the answer/my Nigga
You ain't with the shits/Nigga
Your Daddy raised a bitch/my Nigga
I swear you dark as shit/Nigga

They don't care about us/my Nigga
They don't even see us/my nigga
We might as well all be dead/my Nigga
The banks are too big to fail/my Nigga
Then we too small to win/my Nigga
Give me another hit/my Nigga
We could run this area/Nigga
You trying to get rich/my Nigga?

MOTHER
You're worth so much more than/that word
Your soul sings a beautiful song of art, worth more than/that word
I want to hear those songs not/that word
I better not hear it in my house/that word
If that's all you say that's all you'll be is/that word
I don't want your brother using/that word
These rappers use it to keep you ignorant, enough with/that word
It is always demeaning never endearing/that word
It's only an insult/that word
It's not ours to claim/that word
Covered in blood and suffering is/that word
You cage yourself with/that word

Bone

warmth beneath skin it was
warm beneath your skin anytime
when winds would twist and dance
beneath your skin a hiding place.
nothing left standing on
barren lands and fruitless trees
warmth was your breath
mere memory ignites you
no match or equal.
smothered on cold days
burn bright and quick
burn half as bright twice as quick
before it was let it burn
better it be extinguished
best if dark
beneath spectacle no soul.
morning stained by
sleet and snow morning memories
stained by last night
not the same one from before
that was ages ago
a different person now
old skin
a heap on the floor
shed that skin of persona
shed skin of self
we are more than skin bone and tissue
sin is nothing but flesh unless
more can be shown

more can be shown from flesh
and bone mash and mangle
gnash teeth and bone
pile bone as you do leaves
do not leave but jump in
tear flesh from bone and hear
a rattle that echoes.

Travelogue

going on tubes of
metal through
the sky hoping to crash-land
and assign nationalities to
our problems wishing
that they take one-way
tickets to never trouble
us again but
issues only take round
trips

Goodnight at Dawn

july days
made lukewarm by your frozen demeanor
ending days over toast
saying good night at dawn
stuck in mournful joy
static clarity wheezing through speakers
so much was said in silence
muted tvs turning depp into chaplin
placing the past in the present
i could never move forward
your face bathed in dull blue light

Unwashed Reused

  seventy percent water
     thirty percent falsehood
         that's what we are
             through arteries and veins
                rocks and ravines
                   gravity pushed us down further.
                        at the impasse we separated
                speak now, wave current
            whisper across a distance:
     without you
all skies
are second hand
     twice worn, unwashed, reused.

The Shrinking

taking the road well-traveled
I am taken
my worn-out soles crying out in pain
from slamming concrete
cosmic traveler moves beyond
and well outside of myself
shrunken down thrown in the oasis of blankets
swimming through sweat
sliding down the blanket down to the floor
using my hands and feet to break my fall
through the gaps   between my bedroom door and floor I ran
through the cracks of apartments from unit to unit
household to household seeing the lives of so many
seeing that no one is unique
hearing their arguments illuminated
through the pale light of screens
watch world, watch us watch ourselves
street level and shrunken, made to shrink at the enormity of concrete
    blocks
glass buildings scratching the sky's back
mountains of tires   barely escaping
their rubber avalanche
roar of the outside
blaring horns
dodging sudden death   feet overhead
palms over ears, no shelter from the noise storm
the only reprieve was below
down in the depths deeper
into the gaps of sewer grates

the churn of noise muffled

now but the falling

deeper
        into the cavern

underneath
      the world of the city falling   downward into that shaft
85 million liters of wet
further down I fell
      here was a freedom in the falling
better to fall

The Dream

two silent riders arrive at the ruined tower
cascade of decaying stones falls over heads
a summit littered by children, half-dressed and fully bloated
no words only thousand-yard stares

where is he?
where is he?

sunken eyes avoid his own
no words only dirt-stained fingers
pointing onward.
rubble and remains litter the path

where is he?

on all four he crawled towards them
with skin as dark as his own, he saw
more beast than man
arm and leg shift in
unison

dressed in dirt he crawled over to the second rider
sniffing shyly at his fingers
but bore only sharp white daggers towards the first rider
the beast bore a face like his own
the first rider turned away

to the window, he fled for a reprieve
the first rider spews thick black bile as his body trembles
there it stood tall and proud in ancient power
tree taller than the ruined tower they occupied

leaves of emerald and branches thick as his body
so large the wind became its subject
defiant in stationary power
on each branch balloons darker than black

Willowridge Towers (God Speak)

the place I
once lived had
three towers
Richgrove Drive
lined with
houses my
mother would
never own
my Nike backpack held
drawings, crayons and issues
I hadn't named
the end of
the street
felt like
the end of
the world where
my mother
rented ten thousand
residents half
of them cockroaches

Taharqa

the kings of old Egypt
with skins as dark as mine wrap his body in gold
fill his ears with lead
scrape brain from skull with spoon
he must be presentable
the face of the king must be open
soon he meets
the lord of the horizon
time is the vast sky
leaps into it wide open
his new wings grow
rip bone and tissue with pride
they must emerge
the falcon returns the sky

Clutter

all day spent clearing clutter out of open spaces
my old figure drawings with wrong gesture and wrong anatomy
"Never throw out your old work," Mrs Yarmol once said

I pull memories out of hidden spaces

make open space a thing of the past
with each item I am back into the past
gym class dodgeball Dragon Ball Z

with some memories left hidden

birds of prey

do you remember the days we spent
your florescent room listening
to david attenborough
his voice escaping through smoke
you know, hawks are the only birds of prey that hunt in packs?

cloaked in red you snorted in agreement

1:26 AM

if we could remake ourselves
we would choose more rationality
surely
despite our better judgment
our dreams slip
passing time makes them impossible
waves and shores are lovers
yet we intervene with feeble sandcastles
it hurts
they never say how much
it hurts

if we could remake ourselves
we would choose more compassion
surely
born alone and buried alone
but cannot live without each other
paradox of purpose
our shared anathema
the Aztecs knew
the whole of one's heart
fits in one whole hand

Field Notes on the Hermit

I hiked throughout the valley making sure to be as silent as possible
my ankles and arms marked by mosquito bites
my hair permanently plastered on my forehead.

It was on the third day when I saw him

the hermit sits among battered branches
white bark rubbing off on green grass
his pale feet covered by the dirt of the forest

red leaves falling at each stroke of his paintbrush
wine-soaked leaves stain his fingertips
I observed the hermit either painting or writing
often in the shade of the trees

submerged in solitary stillness
unaware I watched him
looking down to only make field notes
no release valve
pressure of silence envelopes him

the hermit has made his bargain with the forest
a man who chose to isolate himself all these years
from his friends and family
all others sacrificed for solace
why?

no vacancies in this wood
all parts filled by him
his body covered in a mess of green leaves, rotten clothing and blankets
a hat a tangle of grass held together by thin branches

the scent of fresh earth clung to him radiated off him
his heartbeat interwound with the forest
her branches spiral around his body
his disguise merged him with the wood

I traveled on the narrow paths worn by his feet
no space for betrayal on moss-covered paths
these mountains, this wood; calm and unyielding

a constant giver of sustenance, warmth, shelter
in my journey through the forest
I was surrounded by her emerald frock
I must imagine the hermit is happy

there is no demand the forest makes of you
she is the forever-giving partner
intimate with each river, valley and flows
none more welcoming than shapely ravines

every part of the hermit is stitched on her green dress
surrounded by salvation

Stillness

Wisps of striding cloud conceal all
but the sight of the sun

accompanied by two bowed heads
revealing all in the face of the altar

elk sear through snow from the mountain spine
with not even a shrug at their presence

Familiar Tale

the soldiers killed us with the relentless fire of machine guns
their bodies recoiling in ecstasy

lined up shoulder to shoulder facing the river
we fell backwards and were swallowed whole
water made thick with our blood
soil ate our bodies and bore fruits of wrath
the smell of my home hung in my nose
my mother and father hung in my nose
women whispered for their children
and children whined long into that night
their voices rang tickling the leaves of trees
the survivors crawled caked in blood and pity

the soldiers ran them down and kept score
each life extinguished with bayonets
their laughter swallowed us whole
awash in moonlight revealed the beast within
a sight so unbearable

Around the Fire

I could feel the wet through my clothes
through my skin and in my veins
you held me in your arms and I still froze

the night air grabbing at my bones, shaking them
I sought shelter under you

you pulled the tarp off your skin
wincing as flesh strands split from plastic

your skin became my refuge
the last escape from shooting rain

you stretched your flesh tent over me
cold metal pins stabbing the warm corners of your skin

piercing goosebumps, body hair, and earth
all
just to keep me dry

Standard Repertoire of the Immigrant Genre

the same standards that turned an artist in his own country
to a chauffeur in mine.

he had his watercolor dreams shapely and pink
his concepts blooming like
wild orchids
white petals smeared across the concrete by the reality that
if he does not secure capital
his children go hungry
he is five years over 35. those grants don't apply anymore
doesn't have a reference for the New Immigrant Artist Grant
those concepts from his mind's eye
were once as detailed as textiles from *Zanjan*, exploding in colour
now muted, shrunken and obscured by the veil of
overdraft, declined, past due, compound interest

the same standards that turned a musician in his own country
to a delivery boy in mine.

the notes are unknown to him
but his movements adjust to the standard repertoire
no words only rhythm in his knock
gift-wrapping chart-topping fast food
his in-app profile picture fades just like
the faces of all the others we reduced
he does gigs here just like back home
at the cultural centre or the bar downtown,
owned by another immigrant from Kerala
exhausted by his other jobs yet he fights to keep hearing the notes

each pluck on his sitar gives him new life
your family or your passion?
the music in his head drowned by the shrieking of
rent, late fees, service charge, eviction

The Assistant Manager

He knew a little bit about everything. The Assistant Manager could speak on Mourinho's Inter
    soccer team, Lucky Dube, and the ins and outs of tractors.

My sister, and I were his team and we were well coached. Weekend shopping trips to
    Woodbine, Sherway, Sheridan, and Bramelea, the venue did not matter. We always
    won.

He was more tactically aware than the soccer *experts* on The Score and TSN. I would tell him
    to audition and show them up. He would laugh it off, as he did most things I said.

He would tell it to you straight. No need for bells or whistles. He would tell it to you straight.
    The way you had to hear it, a firm voice from a warm smile.

He wasn't as serious as the Navigator, humour and sarcasm held his frame together.
    I held hope that I would reach his six feet. (I didn't)

I remember seeing his broad shoulders go down our hallway. Headed to work while I slipped
    out of a dream. Night shift and I never once heard him complain. Not once. He taught
        me that manhood was about keeping your word and doing the thing, no matter
            how hard.

He felt like what I imagined an older brother would be. The Assistant
Manager would slip
    secret five-dollars bills here and there. *2.50 each,* he would say.

I would spend my share as soon as I got it, straight to the Tuck Shop
for $2 surprise bags. You
    never knew what each one would be. When I hovered above the
striped blue and white bags I was in destiny's hands.

You could rip the paper and staples of your bag and look inside first.
I never did.
    I would always stick my hand in and pull out each item. I
loved being caught off guard.

    Leukemia
        Radiation
            St Micheals

I didn't know what these things were.

I wanted to put them back in the surprise bag and staple it shut. I
wanted to hand that bag
    back to the Tuck Shop owner and never carry it home with me.
The Assistant Manager

was big and indestructible. I felt like a titan on his shoulders. He went
from stocky and strong
    to rail thin and weak. His shoulders were no longer travel
options.

I learned that cancer had a scent. I could smell it on him. The scent
couldn't be washed away.
    not even with my mother's tears.

She would go back and forth.

St Michaels and home
Home then St Micheals

How could something so bad happen to someone so good?

Mother took care of her brother. Like how my older sister would take care of me.

We no longer got into formation for our shopping trips. When I would go see the Assistant
    Manager he was a prisoner of his bed, immobile, with gaunt cheeks.

His hospital room was separated in half with a thin curtain. The smell of the bedpan from
    the other side hung in my nose and stayed there each subway ride home.

His shoulders had become narrower and his whole frame was held together by resilience
    beaten down by radiation. He looked as small as a child under that hospital blanket.

I hated seeing the Assistant Manager looking that weak.

I was so scared for him, imagine how scared he must have been. Yet each time we went to
St Micheals, he greeted me with a smile.

We couldn't speak for hours about Arsenal and Manchester United anymore. He got tired faster
    and I would have to leave his bedside sooner than I would have liked.

Yet despite the smell and his condition, he still teased my sister and me, putting smiles on our
> faces. He was the brightness peaking through the dark curtain that enveloped us.

His surprise bag was the worst one you could pick out but he remained as resilient as
> Mourinho's Inter team. He never felt sorry for himself, he defied destiny he taught me
> that.

At last he had broken free from that hospital bed, his body responded well to the treatment. The
> sarcasm-filled shopping trips with my sister came back. We were a winning team again.

Despite all he had been through he held no bitterness. Not an ounce of anger radiated off him.

He taught me so much by not even speaking. He taught me the value of having a role model who wasn't as formal as the Navigator.

I realized later he had never been weak. The Assistant Manager remained strong the whole
> time.

Walk Hard

he weighed a little over 75 pounds, light
each step he took to school felt heavy

every step a struggle with his cinderblock shoes
buried deep in his jansport

complexes he had not yet named but strained his back
he kept it all inside, inside his bag, inside his classrooms

he was always on time, homework done on time
but those weights didn't disappear

they crawled out of his bag and into his ears
shoved under his skin, his skin a shield and a target

his skin a uniform he never ordered
used to paint him with a dark broad brush

the place he lived in was the brand for the rest of his life
the sweat from his father's brow dripped to change that story

the tears on his mother's face shed to change that story
their struggle each day to change the story he told about himself

the night shifts, the arguments, the imperfect but stable union a
    counter narrative
all this done to make those steps feel a little lighter

Here Lies a Brother, Friend, and Son

      I couldn't recognize myself in the mirror
            I cleaned and cleaned it
    Who was that? He doesn't look familiar
                I tried to talk to God but he can't hear me
  the demons were laughing too loud

I scarred my body just to
              feel something.
  Surrounded by thousands but totally
Alone
    Now I sit here in this home surrounded by misshapen glass
          All this glass
              all *this dirty* glass
         I want to vanish
  my face twisted by the glass
           a part of me died in that house

Father

I understand what you are feeling, son,
you're not the only one to have the empty.
I've felt that way many times and plenty.
You need to start sleeping early
it's good for your health, your mind, and inner self
This is the fourth time you've called me this week.
I will have the same advice for you every time we speak.
Have you brought your Bible?
Have you been reading it?
Talk to God, son,
the loneliness and the boredom you feel is the devil testing you.
Don't let him win.

Sister

. . . this is the third time you've called me this week
I have my own life, you know
Not like a few years ago, we're not the same kids
I can't hang out with you now
You have all your friends there with you,
why don't you spend time with them?
There is no need to suffer alone
I don't like the idea of sitting around doing nothing.
Join a club or find someone to talk too. There must counselors
If you don't reach out, how can they help you?
Anyway I have to leave now I have thi-

Mother

it's the second time you've called me this week
Next year I want you here
When you are miserable I can feel it too
I never wanted to leave you there
You'd be more than welcome back
you have nothing to prove
you can't mutilate yourself for pride
Have you been eating fruits and vegeta-

Friend

Where do you even live again?
That's way too far, everyone lives closer to the-
We can't really wait for you to arrive just spend time wi-
Sorry I've got to-

(Untitled)

Day
Dozens of feet tiptoe towards the exit
Whispers and hushed words of conversations fly past
Sounds of joyous success and crippling failure
Half heard in cell phone conversations
Lovers, friends, employees, employers, acquaintances, sisters, brothers, mothers, fathers, sons, daughters

I heard them all

The cold draft from the metro crawls across my skin
I move in with the herd shuffling mindlessly towards the Promised Land.
The shepherd at the front of the pack leads them onward. Am I the savior?
I look straight ahead, blind to them. My ears filled with lyrical profanities,
Deaf to them
Their bodies shove me this way and that, hitting me without any thought.

I push them all

I sense them all

Night
That night they arrived. I sensed them; I heard them all
I tried to push them
Spirits or demons? Angels is what I want to believe

A presence in my mind, I can hear thoughts
Vile and cruel with words not of my own
It says to me harsh and unforgiving:

You are worthless you are the son of slaves
They liked you better in boxes and a cage
You hate your own, still a slave to your mind
The mentality of servitude consumes you and your kind
That's why you shoot each other

An apex predator, you and your brothers
The schools didn't teach you the mystery of your people
Now black history turns to black misery
The Black death—

Your wrong I cried, all day every moment, I try
I am a credit to my race a beacon a shining example
I don't need you or another to justify me—

Silly child you have no future, you're no example
Martin Luther Malcolm X you don't even have a sample
Of the integrity that they possessed
You're distressed no matter how hard you try

Your opium is your rap, reality tv and your "ball"
You're just another one of them; you're no different from them at all.
Give yourself to me offer yourself up. I'll love you
I'll accept you
Give into the temptation its so easy
I'll give you any woman you want classy or sleazy
The path is short and rewarding its filled with gold
Just give me that little thing to hold

Your shining light your
Soul.
Don't dismiss me I've been doing double shifts
Lemme strike your heart I won't miss
Don't even start with that. His story is Fiction
He didn't die for you no one could stick by his convictions.
Shhh just listen

I choose my father not you. You're a twisted thing warped by sin
You look like me but you're just a cheap copy
The worst parts of me are in you
You're an inferior warlock I won't drink your brew
I don't **want** your fool's gold
My soul is my life's fire it won't be bought or sold
I am man my own man I'm not in your control

Martin was tested
Malcolm was tested
Siddhartha was tested
Krishna was tested
I Won't be tempted

The creature receded then blinded by light
I crawled back deeper into the recesses of my mind
Black tide kept at bay

Myths Matter

why do I have to choose
realms of
myth or matter
why can't I have both
nothing more than
myth you said
it really didn't matter
myths matter
yet eyes pressed upon me
gaze transfigured into
a burden pressed
upon me like Sisyphus's,
solid stone

you are my burden
I wanted to fix you
reshape shingle to sculpture
yet I don't know how
they carved stone
in those old days
you are a collective of
cracks from your
old days
hard as fact
is your stare
hard as iron
is your stare
you are my burden
a look so mighty

hard to lift
in the realms of
myth and matter
maybe it's easier?

The Arrival

Disturbed us from that view above
We are disturbed by that beam
Who would dare to shine that beam
Directly at us, shooting through the trees

Who would dare to interrupt our gentle sway
Our rhythmic response to the call of the wind

That beam brighter than any light seen across the wood
We speak to our ancestors through the tree rings
They have never seen such

That violent beam swallowed whole that human creature
Lifted him towards the sky and heated our bark

My brothers and I smoking
Smoke from bark billowing into the sky
The beam shoots through all

We rule this wood how dare you.

What Forever Looks Like

Food staining your shirt
grease on your chin
cats standing at attention
waiting for a nibble
this is what forever looks like

TV dinners on trays of aged newspaper
the space on the couch next to you
smaller and smaller
this is what forever looks like

Thin wispy branches of youth
turned to thick aged trunks
rooted in soil
rooted in our high school uniforms
ill-fitting
this is what forever looks like

New Ones Old

another night spent with another girl
another phase of renewal
treating new girls like the old ones
wishing old ones were more like the new
all the contacts in your phone starting to blur

seated in shadow with a new girl among used furniture
darkness illuminated only by intention
shrieking with our internal mouths
wordless warnings piercing fat silence
daring not to reveal how lonely you really were

ensuring your aloofness remained intact
this wasn't love or anything silly
love is weakness
love is needy
you refused to need anyone
you vowed never to get hurt
refusing to reveal your pain
just sailing onward together at a distance

ignoring floodlight, sidelight
steering our shared steel ship straight to mist
ropes of union tighten with each movement
no life left in these rafts

DANIEL MALUKA is a Toronto-based artist and writer born in South Africa. His work takes an Afrocentric approach and incorporates surrealist elements to bring out what lurks in the deep recesses of the mind into the forefront of his work.

DANIEL MALUKA is a Toronto-based artist and writer born in South Africa. His work takes an Afrocentric approach and incorporates surrealist elements to bring out what lurks in the deep recesses of the mind into the forefront of his work.